CHILDREN OF THE KINGDOM

Joyce Good Reis

THOMAS NELSON PUBLISHERS
Nashville

Published in Nashville, Tennessee, by Thomas Nelson, Inc., Publishers, and distributed in Canada by Word Communications, Ltd., Richmond, British Columbia, and in the United Kingdom by Word (UK), Ltd., Milton Keynes, England.

Unless otherwise noted, Scripture quotations are from the *Good News Bible,* Old Testament © 1976 by the American Bible Society; New Testament © 1966, 1971, 1976 American Bible Society. Used by permission.

Scripture quotations noted RSV are from the REVISED STANDARD VERSION of the Bible. Copyright © 1946, 1952, 1971, 1973 by the Division of Christian Education of the National Council of the Churches of Christ in the U.S.A. Used by permission.

Library of Congress Cataloging-in-Publication Data

Reis, Joyce Good.
    Children of the kingdom : a collection of children's sermons / Joyce Good Reis.
    ISBN 0-7852-8293-9
    1. Children's sermons. I. Title.
BV4315.R385 1994
252'.53—dc20
93-34918
CIP

Printed in the United States of America
1 2 3 4 5 6 7 - 00 99 98 97 96 95 94

*To Paul, Shawn, Jeremy, Heather, and Megan
who have taught me what it means to be a
Child of the Kingdom*

Acknowledgments

Most of my stories come from everyday life, from my childhood, and from the lives and experiences of others who have shared themselves with me. Frequently, they do not even know how much they have enriched my life and those of the children who hear their stories. My thanks for their inspiration and encouragement go to my mother, Judy, Phil, Jeanne, Jim, Jenny, John, Mary, Anne, David, Rod and Linda McClarnon, and Art Fothergill.

Contents

AUTUMN

Introduction

———

> At that time the disciples came to Jesus, saying, "Who is the greatest in the kingdom of heaven?"
>
> And calling to him a child, he put him in the midst of them, and said, "Truly, I say to you, unless you turn and become like children, you will never enter the kingdom of heaven. Whoever humbles himself like this child, he is the greatest in the kingdom of heaven."
>
> (Matt. 18:1–4 RSV)

When my youngest daughter was five years old she came to me and told me proudly, "I know why God created me."

I was eager for her explanation. In my mind, I ran through the answers I had learned when I was a child, "God created me to love him and to worship him. God created me in his image and likeness. God has a special plan for my life."

Megan's answer was far simpler and more profound than mine, "He knew you needed a five-year-old to love you."

She was so right.

God made each of us because he knew we need each other in order to share his love with each other. He uses us to love and he uses us to teach. That is the reason I enjoy talking with you children, and sharing God with you.

The Pueblo Indians of the Southwestern United States believe that wisdom is found in the young and the old who are both closest to the hand of God. I, too, find that children have unique gifts. You have a simple faith in God which helps you to understand what we adults often question. Frequently, I turn to you with my questions rather than answers so that I might learn from you and with you. To you belongs the Kingdom of God. To you belongs the gift of sharing that kingdom with the rest of us.

To you, parents, pastors, teachers, and adults who love children, no matter how these simple lessons are presented, they all provide an opportunity to share the teachings of Christ in everyday terms as Jesus himself taught. While these messages can be used in junior church or as part of a children's program, when they are included in the regular Sunday morning service, they involve the child in worship. These lessons are meant both for children and the child in all of us.

Feel free to adapt the stories and examples to your own experiences and memories. The more personal the better since children love hearing about the experiences and childhoods of adults they know. These sermons may inspire different lessons than the ones I have suggested or you may find a different scripture verse to accompany your own message. I use props for some of the lessons because seeing some everyday object helps the children relate to and remember the lesson. I sing in the choir and, therefore, wear a choir robe when I share the children's moments. No one will ever forget the morning I wore roller skates beneath my robe for a message about a skating accident I had!

Props can sometimes include something the children may take home with them, but don't feel you must provide something every Sunday, especially if you have as many children as we do at our services. Be sure to include instructions for proper use of whatever you give the children. For example, cookies should be saved until church is over;

paper wrapped around a piece of candy needs to be thrown away in the proper place; etc. The items also need to be appropriate for all age groups. Our children's message time includes children from toddlers to sixth grade. A piece of candy with instructions to hold it until after the service might not be appreciated by a toddler's mother who will have to persuade the little one to wait.

When you plan a children's sermon, consider where you will be and where the children are to sit. I prefer to sit on a step with the children, but I have to admit it isn't easy getting up gracefully in a choir robe or a dress while juggling a soccer ball or an armful of stuffed animals. Some churches use a small chair or stool for the speaker. There is value in being at the same level as the children. You can establish eye contact, involve them in conversation, and better control the wiggles when you are in their midst. I sit down with them, encourage them to hold my prop, take a squirmer onto my lap, and speak to them. Even though the message is enjoyed by all ages, it is especially intended for the little ones and they need to know that they are the focus of attention for that few minutes.

How long should the message be? The average attention span of children in Sunday best clothes, in front of a congregation, away from a watchful mom and dad, is three to five minutes. My sermons are short. I illustrate a point, usually only one, state the point, and then repeat it, frequently in a prayer at the end. I try to involve the children with a question. I share with them experiences to which they can relate and challenge them to think of similar events in their own lives. Since I know many of them by name, it is easy to ask about a new baby in the family, or how things are going at school, but again, we keep such conversations brief, usually lasting as long as it takes for the last one to come forward and sit down.

The children's message should complement the entire service. I achieve this by keeping focused to one idea, brief and to the point. I rarely coordinate my lessons with those of the pastor's sermon or the lectionary lesson, but somehow, that frequently happens anyway. Often, I have a prepared message written on index cards, but as I get ready for church on Sunday morning, or perhaps in the car driving to church, the Spirit speaks to me and another lesson comes to mind. Prayer and meditation provide many an idea for children's messages, as well as blessing the time spent with the children.

Most important to children's messages is a genuine love for the children who have a special place in Jesus' heart. You don't have to be a parent. You don't have to be a preacher. You don't even have to have a "gift" for relating to little ones. You only need to love them and to want to share God and his kingdom with them.

ADVENT

1

MORE TO COME

But they who wait for the LORD shall renew their strength, they shall mount up with wings like eagles, they shall run and not be weary, they shall walk and not faint.

(Isa. 40:31 RSV)

What's the hardest part of Christmas? It's the waiting. I know how hard it is to wait for Christmas. You wait for Christmas just as the Hebrew people waited for the Savior to come. For hundreds of years they waited. Imagine you are a young shepherd on a hillside tending your flock. At night, you gather with other shepherds around a fire to stay warm and you listen to the stories the others tell. There's no television. They talk about David, a boy who took on a giant with nothing but a slingshot. They tell about Gideon and Samson and Daniel and Joshua. These men are all heroes, and their stories are very familiar to you. The stories of the Hebrew people never ended with, "They lived happily ever after." Their stories always ended with, "There's more to come." They waited for the Savior.

Advent is the time of the year when we prepare for the coming of Christ as a baby in a manger. We light candles to remind us "there's more to come." Advent is a time of waiting, just as the Hebrew people waited. How should we wait? What should we do?

Isaiah, one of the heroes the shepherds would share stories about, wrote, "They who wait for the LORD shall renew their strength, they shall mount up with wings like eagles, they shall run and not be weary, they shall walk and not faint" (Isa. 40:31 RSV).

Waiting is not meant to be a time of sitting and doing nothing. There is a great deal of activity in Isaiah's words: soaring like an eagle, running, walking. You're supposed to be busy while waiting. Not busy for the sake of busy-ness, but busy about the work of the Lord. Waiting and working.

Preparing a place in your heart for the Baby Jesus. You know the story's ending—the Baby Jesus did come and will come in your hearts again at the end of Advent. And still the ending's the same: "There's more to come," because Jesus did promise he will return.

2

THE BIRDS

The attitude you should have is the one that Christ Jesus had:

He always had the nature of God, but he did not think that by force he should try to become equal with God.

Instead of this, of his own free will he gave up all he had, and took the nature of a servant.

He became like man and appeared in human likeness.

(Phil. 2:5–7)

There is a story about a family preparing to go to church on Christmas Eve. The mother and children were ready to leave when the father announced he would not be going. The mother wanted the whole family to go together, but the father argued that he did not believe in Jesus. The father told her that it did not make sense to him that God would become a man. So, sadly, the mother and the children went without the father, while he settled down in his favorite chair to read a book.

He heard a noise at the window and went to investigate. It was snowing very hard outside and getting colder. A flock of birds gathered in his yard and one of them, attracted by the lights in the house, had accidentally flown into the window. They must be cold and maybe hungry, the father thought. Perhaps I could open the barn door and let them in there out of the weather.

He put on his coat and scarf and gloves and went out to the barn. The birds scattered when he approached them. They flew up to the tree and watched him from there. He opened the barn doors and turned on a small light hanging from the ceiling.

"There, birds, go in and warm up," he shouted.

The birds looked at him, but didn't move. He scattered some birdseed on the barn floor, but they still didn't move. The man went out into the yard and tried to coax them and shoo them into the barn, but they still didn't move. He threw some seed on the ground to form a path to the barn, but the birds still sat. Finally, in exasperation he said aloud, "If only I could become a bird for just a few minutes, I might be able to lead them into the barn to the light, warmth, and food."

Just then, in the distance, the church bells rang. When the man heard them, he realized why Christ had been born: to lead us all to the light. He hurried to church to be with his family.

3
TINSEL

Create in me a clean heart, O God, and put a new and right spirit within me.

(Ps. 51:10 RSV)

Many years ago, there was a mother who was preparing for Christmas. She had baked cookies and made gifts and wrapped them. She put up a Christmas tree in the parlor with the gifts under it, then closed the door to that room so the children couldn't see their gifts. She still had a lot of cleaning to do to get ready for the special day. With many little children and much work to do, she was exhausted by all her chores. She cleaned and cleaned every room in her house, every corner from the basement to the attic. But she missed one little spot behind the Christmas tree, where she couldn't see or reach.

Christmas Eve came and she tucked all the children into bed one by one with a kiss and a story. She was anxious to get to bed herself because she knew the children would be up early to open the doors and see the tree and their gifts. Little did the mother know that while she slept, a small spider made its way out of the corner behind the tree, the very spot the mother hadn't cleaned. The little spider was very curious about the Christmas tree. He had never seen one before. He climbed all the way to the top and looked down, then he slid all the way to the bottom. He raced from side to side, bouncing from one branch to another. He smiled at himself in the silvery balls and inspected each and every ornament. Of course, everywhere the spider went, he spun a web. Before the night was over, he had covered the tree with spider webs.

There was another visitor that night after the spider had returned to his corner. The Lord came. He noticed how clean the house was and how hard the mother had worked to prepare for Christmas. He also saw what the spider had done and even though the Lord admired the little spider, he knew the mother would be most upset when she saw the web. So, Jesus turned the spider web into silver.

The tinsel of a Christmas tree reminds you of this story. No matter how hard you work to prepare your hearts for the coming of the Lord, it is he who makes your efforts worthwhile. He comes into your hearts and touches every corner. He takes your mistakes and changes them into something precious.

4

GIFTS FOR A BABY

They went into the house, and when they saw the child with his mother Mary, they knelt down and worshiped him. They brought out their gifts of gold, frankincense, and myrrh, and presented them to him.

(Matt. 2:11)

Because this is the Christmas season, I've been thinking about gifts to get for a new baby. Perhaps a teething ring, or a stuffed animal, or a pair of booties. Those are all things a baby can use. I might also get something for the mother to use for the baby, like lotion or diapers. These are practical gifts every baby needs. When you think about gifts you might get a new baby, it makes the Magi's gifts to the Baby Jesus seem very strange.

Gold, frankincense, and myrrh for a baby? Not gifts I would consider. But to the Magi, these gifts made great sense. Gold was the gift one would give a king. It was precious, valuable, the only gift one could offer a king. Frankincense was a wood that when burned produced a fragrant smoke. It was used in the temple, and the smoke was believed to be pleasing to God. Frankincense was the gift one would offer God. Myrrh was a very expensive perfumed oil. It was used to prepare a body after death. It was a gift one would give a grown person.

The Magi honored the Baby Jesus as a king, as the Son of God, and as a man. No baby rattles or blue blankets, but three gifts that acknowledged who this baby was.

WINTER

5

NEW YEAR'S RESOLUTIONS

Rejoice in each day as the psalm tells you:

This is the day of the LORD's victory; let us be
happy, let us celebrate!

(Ps. 118:24)

Have you ever made New Year's resolutions? Those are promises you make to yourself about what you plan to do better in the new year. You might make resolutions to make your bed every day, or take more baths or help with the dishes or get better grades. Usually resolutions are things you think you should do, but don't really want to do. The problem with resolutions is they rarely last till the end of January.

This year, you might want to make resolutions and share them with someone. That way, the person can help you keep your resolutions.

First, give yourself the gift of time. When you learn to live each day as it comes, you don't have time to worry about yesterday or tomorrow. Enjoy each day.

Give yourself the gift of love. Make a resolution to make more friendships by first being a friend to others.

Give yourself the gift of fun by relaxing and enjoying life. You may not need to be reminded of this, but make a resolution to share your smiles and jokes and laughter with your family and friends.

Give yourself the gift of others. Make a resolution to give and receive from others. That's all a part of loving.

Give yourself the gift of joy. Rejoice in what you have rather than wanting what you really don't need.

6

THE OLD SHOEMAKER

Whoever does what my Father in heaven wants him to do is my brother, my sister, and my mother.
(Matt. 12:50)

There was an old shoemaker who lived many years ago. Every night he prayed for the same thing, to see the Lord before he died. One night, an angel appeared to him and told him his prayer would be answered: the next day, the Lord would visit him. He was so excited he could not sleep. He cleaned his small shoe shop and prepared a pot of stew and made a new pair of fine leather shoes for the Lord.

When morning came, the old man looked out his window to find a fresh snowfall. It was so deep that people were having difficulty making their way down the street. He saw someone huddled over, struggling against the snow and wind. Thinking the person was surely cold, he opened his door and invited her in to warm herself by his fire.

The old woman was very cold and eagerly accepted his invitation. The shoemaker offered her a bowl of stew. She had not eaten that day and was pleased to eat his stew. Before he knew it, he had given her all the stew. Now he had none left for the Lord, but he still had the shoes. The woman finished the meal and left, and the shoemaker settled down to wait for the Lord.

The snow continued to fall heavily and as evening approached the shoemaker began to lose heart. Surely the Lord would not come, he thought. Then there was a knock at his door and he opened it to find a young woman standing there shivering. When he invited her in, he noticed she carried a bundle. Wrapped inside was a small baby. The mother explained she had come a long way and had further to go.

"See," she told him, "I have even worn a hole in the bottom of my shoe."

The shoemaker returned the baby to his mother's arms. "I can help," he said, "for I am the best shoemaker in the town."

The young mother protested she did not have the money to pay for shoes, but the man insisted she take them anyway. "I made them for someone special, but it appears he won't be by to pick them up," he told her.

The shoes fit perfectly and while she put them on, the shoemaker found a small pair for the baby also. She wrapped the baby up in his blanket and thanked the man and they left. The old man was very disappointed; the Lord had not come. Perhaps the weather kept him away. Or maybe the shop wasn't good enough.

That night in his evening prayers, the shoemaker asked, "Why didn't you come, Lord?"

From the darkness came an answer, "But I did come. I was hungry and cold and you fed me. I was poor and you clothed me."

7

IT SNOWED IN SAUDI ARABIA

Come, let us praise the LORD! Let us sing for joy to God, who protects us! Let us come before him with thanksgiving and sing joyful songs of praise. For the LORD is a mighty God, a mighty king over all the gods. He rules over the whole earth, from the deepest caves to the highest hills. He rules over the sea, which he made; the land also, which he himself formed.

(Ps. 95:1–5)

I have childhood friends who were teachers in Saudi Arabia. When you think of Saudi Arabia, you usually think of deserts and camels and very hot weather. My friends frequently told their children, who were born and raised in Saudi Arabia, about the fun they had when they were children when it snowed. My friends and I would all go sledding and build snow forts and have snowball fights. We ice-skated and scooped up bowls of snow for snow ice cream.

My friends' children could not understand this. It is very difficult to imagine snow when you live in a desert. One year, however, the winter was unusually cold and there was a freak storm. It actually snowed in Saudi Arabia! My friends' children were afraid to go out in it at first. They thought it might hurt them. There wasn't enough snow for sledding, but they did make a snowball and throw it.

Sometimes, God comes to you in an unexpected way. You may be surprised and afraid. You can't imagine what he wants or what you're supposed to do. You might not be prepared for his presence. You might even need to search your memory for the last time he came in this way. God's surprises are often fun, and you can enjoy something as unique and simple as a snowfall in Saudi Arabia.

8

TEAM JESUS

Whatever you do, work at it with all your heart, as though you were working for the Lord and not for men. Remember that the Lord will give you as a reward what he has kept for his people.

(Col. 3:23–24)

Do you enjoy watching the Olympics every two years? Do you follow all the competitions of Team USA? The Winter Olympics remind me of the church and all the activities that occur there. If your church held an Olympics, what sorts of events might you have?

Perhaps the acolytes could participate in slalom candle-lighting. The choir would have free-style singing, although the director might not be too happy. The piano or organ players specialize in cross-country keyboard playing. The ushers go for the gold, and youth directors need to be as fast as speed skaters to keep up with youth. Jumpers? Just visit the children's choir. Our pastor, standing in the pulpit, knows how to downhill preach.

What about the Olympic flame? It shines brightly for the days of the contests, then is extinguished until the next Olympics. The tongues of flame above the apostles' heads on Pentecost continue to burn in today's church because our flame is an eternal one.

Team Jesus is open to you. It doesn't have tryouts and it doesn't limit itself to a few of the best. You might find a place in a Sunday school class or in a children's choir or in a youth group or in a junior bells choir or on a sports team. Jesus asks you to give your all, not for two weeks of competition or for four years but for every day of your life. The best part of Team Jesus is that events are held daily and weekly, not just for a few days once every two years.

Athletes concentrate, practice, and devote their time and energy, giving up other activities and work for years. Their rewards—if the athletes are the best—are a piece of metal and a few minutes of glory. Team Jesus' reward is eternal glory. Just give your all and you, too, can make the team.

9

JIGSAW PUZZLES

You are the people of God; he loved you and chose you for his own. So then, you must clothe yourselves with compassion, kindness, humility, gentleness, and patience. Be tolerant with one another and forgive one another whenever any of you has a complaint against someone else. You must forgive one another just as the Lord has forgiven you. And to all these qualities add love, which binds all things together in perfect unity.

(Col. 3:12–14)

Do you like jigsaw puzzles? I do. Every year I buy one for Christmas and my family puts it together. I like the challenge of finding just the right piece and putting it where it belongs and watching as a picture develops. Then when the puzzle is complete, I could use a special glue to save it forever, but I think it is more fun to put it back in its box and do it again another time.

Living as a Christian is like a jigsaw puzzle. Each new experience and each new lesson learned fit together into a beautiful picture. If you take one piece or experience or lesson out of the puzzle and look at it, it might not make sense, because you can't see how it fits in the whole picture. But putting all the pieces together lets you see how each experience or lesson fits in the whole picture of your life.

The Bible lists several pieces of the puzzle that you need to put together to complete the picture of your life. They are: compassion, kindness, humility, gentleness, and patience, tolerance of others, forgiveness, and thankfulness.

With the help of your friends, you can find the pieces of your puzzle and put them together to show a rich picture of the working of God in your life. Then, you can add the glue of Christ's love, and the puzzle pieces of your life will be bound together in peace and harmony.

10

SIGNS OF GOD'S LOVE

I am putting my bow in the clouds. It will be the sign of my covenant with the world. Whenever I cover the sky with clouds and the rainbow appears, I will remember my promise to you and to all the animals that a flood will never again destroy all living beings. When the rainbow appears in the clouds, I will see it and remember the everlasting covenant between me and all living beings on earth.

(Gen. 9:13–16)

My daughter came home from college for Christmas with a bad case of laryngitis. You may have had such a bad cold and sore throat that you, too, lost your voice, so you know how she felt. The doctor told her she shouldn't even try to whisper or she might lose her voice for weeks. She was so desperate to talk with us, especially since she had been away from home and had much to share with us. She couldn't sing the Christmas carols which were her favorite songs. She couldn't talk on the phone to friends she hadn't seen in months. On top of all this, she didn't feel well. She was miserable!

Fortunately, she remembered a little sign language which we had learned a few years earlier when her youngest sister had hearing problems. We all waited patiently and tried our best to understand her signs and finger spellings. And within a week her voice returned.

The week reminded me of how God communicates with us through signs. We want so much to be able to hear his voice that we frequently don't look for the signs of what he wants to tell us.

Remember the story of Noah? After the flood had destroyed everything except the animals and people on the ark, God told Noah that God would never again send the flood waters to destroy the earth. As a sign of this promise made to Noah, God said, "I am putting my bow in the clouds. It will be the sign of my covenant with the world. Whenever I cover the sky with clouds and the rainbow appears, I will remember my promise to you and to all the animals that a flood will never again destroy all living beings. When the rainbow appears in the clouds, I will see it and remember the everlasting covenant between me and all living beings on earth" (Gen. 9:13–16).

The rainbow is not the only sign of God's love. Look around you every day and see what signs you can find—perhaps the smile of a friend or a beautiful sunset or the unfolding of a little flower or the purr of a kitten. All around us there are signs of God's love waiting for us to find them.

11

THE CORNERSTONE

You, too, are built upon the foundation laid by the apostles and prophets, the cornerstone being Christ Jesus himself. He is the one who holds the whole building together and makes it grow into a sacred temple dedicated to the Lord.

(Eph. 2:20–21)

Many years ago I lived in an old farmhouse that had a wood-burning stove in the kitchen. I decided to put bricks behind the stove to protect the wall from the heat. Because the stove was in a corner, the bricks had to run along one wall into the corner and then along the other wall, from the floor to the ceiling. I thought I could do the project myself because I had laid bricks for a patio, and it didn't seem to be much more difficult than that.

So I started on one side and put bricks and mortar up one row at a time. I used a level to make sure the bricks were even and the wall straight. But by the time I had laid rows three feet high, the wall was crooked. I tore it down and put it up again and the same thing happened, even though I was very careful and leveled each brick. I finally called a bricklayer and he came and finished the project in one day, while I had been struggling a week to get three feet high!

The bricklayer told me his secret. Instead of starting at one side and working to the other and back again, he began in the corner. He placed the cornerstone first and then ran a row to the two ends. The cornerstone is the most important stone because it sets the course of the wall and makes it run straight.

This experience reminded me that Paul called Christ Jesus a "cornerstone" and the prophet Isaiah wrote, "This, now, is what the Sovereign LORD says: 'I am placing in Zion a foundation that is firm and strong. In it I am putting a solid cornerstone'" (28:16).

Jesus Christ is your cornerstone. With him, your life can be straight and stable. When I used the level I measured from one brick to another to make the wall straight. Looking to other people for direction can make your life as crooked as my wall. Instead, you need to look to Jesus, the cornerstone, to make your wall straight and to join us all together into a holy temple dedicated to the Lord.

12

COINS

Then Jesus said to the disciples, "And so I tell you not to worry about the food you need to stay alive or about the clothes you need for your body. Life is much more important than food, and the body much more important than clothes. Look at the crows: they don't plant seeds or gather a harvest; they don't have storage rooms or barns; God feeds them! You are worth so much more than birds!"

(Luke 12:22–24)

I have friends from different countries and when they visit I ask them for a coin from their homeland. In a short time I have collected a yen from Japan, a kopek from Russia, a peso from Mexico, a quarter from Canada, a pound from England, and coins from Colombia, France, Germany, and Finland. The coins are all different and interesting. They are large and small, six-sided and round, copper and silver and nickel. There are different pictures on each one. They each have value in the country from which they come, but are worthless here. I couldn't go to the store and buy a candy bar with a kopek. I couldn't use a yen in a soda machine or a peso in a pay phone.

In fact, a few years ago a burglar stole some of my coins and made the mistake of trying to buy a package of cigarettes with my Colombian coin and was arrested.

What makes a penny a penny or a dime worth ten pennies? Our government has set the value of our money, just as all the other countries set the value of their coins.

Who sets your value? Who says what you're worth? God does. The God who knew you before you were even born and knows every hair on your head has a plan for your life, holds you in his hands, provides you with a treasure that will never be stolen, and wants to spend an eternity with you. This is the God who gave his only Son just for you. That's how much he values you.

13

PRETZELS

Some people brought children to Jesus for him to place his hands on them and to pray for them, but the disciples scolded the people. Jesus said, "Let the children come to me and do not stop them, because the Kingdom of heaven belongs to such as these."

(Matt. 19:13–14)

When I was a little girl, my great-grand-mother would bake cinnamon rolls every Saturday to have for breakfast after church on Sunday. She usually had a few scraps of dough left over and she would sprinkle cinnamon and sugar on them and bake them as little treats for us. She did this to show us how special she thought we were.

Someone shared with me the story of pretzels which reminded me of the cinnamon-sugar treats. Many centuries ago in Italy, a monk was baking loaves of bread. He gathered together the scraps of dough so as not to waste them and rolled them into long rods which he then twisted into the shape of a child's arms folded in prayer. After these shapes were baked, the monk would give them to children who could say their prayers. He called them *pretiola,* which means "little reward." The monk understood the special place children held in Jesus' heart.

The *pretiola* became famous and others began to bake them as well even as far away as Germany and Austria. The name changed to "bretzel" and then to "pretzel," which is what we still call them. Pretzels became a special treat during the Lenten season when people ate less meat and more breads and pastries.

Adults think the pretzel represents the Trinity because of the three holes, one each for the Father, the Son, and the Holy Spirit. But, as the monk who created them believed, pretzels really remind us that praying children are special to God.

14

YOUR FATHER'S LETTERS

See how much the Father has loved us! His love is so great that we are called God's children.

(1 John 3:1)

This is how we know what love is: Christ gave his life for us.

(1 John 3:16)

We love because God first loved us.

(1 John 4:19)

For God loved the world so much that he gave his only Son, so that everyone who believes in him may not die but have eternal life.

(John 3:16)

I love you just as the Father loves me; remain in my love.

(John 15:9)

When my father died, my mother gave me a letter he wrote for Christmas when I was a baby. He wrote it as if it were my diary. The letter talked about the Christmas tree we had and the bubble lights and shiny balls that I watched all day. My father described the pretty packages under the tree and how I wanted to play with the paper and bows instead of the toys inside. When I finally opened one of the boxes there was a beautiful baby doll. My grandpa gave me a baby buggy and a big toy box. My grandma gave me a new skirt and blouse and white shoes and bedroom slippers with squeaky toes. Santa brought a pounding toy and a top and books.

My father went on to tell what we did that day, how we went for a ride in the car on slippery roads and had dinner at my great-grandparents' house.

Of course, I don't remember this Christmas when I was a baby, and as I grew older it was sometimes hard to remember that my father loved me so much that he took the time to write to me about this event in my early life. He was busy a lot, both at work and at home, and I had my own life later.

Sometimes, your life gets so busy that you lose sight of how much God loves you too. Fortunately, there are letters in the Bible to remind you. One of them tells you, "See how much the Father has loved us! His love is so great that we are called God's children" (1 John 3:1).

And, "This is how we know what love is: Christ gave his life for us" (1 John 3:16).

"We love because God first loved us" (1 John 4:19).

"For God loved the world so much that he gave his only Son, so that everyone who believes in him may not die but have eternal life" (John 3:16).

"I love you just as the Father loves me; remain in my love" (John 15:9).

15

WANTS VERSUS NEEDS

And with all his abundant wealth through Christ
Jesus, my God will supply all your needs.

(Phil. 4:19)

Don't you just love Girl Scout cookies? I do.
Every spring I buy several boxes of thin mint
cookies and peanut butter sandwiches. I'd love to
sit down and eat every single cookie at one time.
But I also like them frozen so I have to put some
in the freezer and wait to eat them. Some years I
have bought extra boxes so I can eat some and
save some. I'm just crazy about these cookies.

But as much as I like Girl Scout cookies, I need to eat other foods as well, to stay healthy and not become fat! I *need* fruits and vegetables and meat and bread. I *want* to eat cookies.

Life is full of decisions between needs and wants. You want lots of toys for Christmas, but sometimes get clothing you need instead. You want to spend your school days playing, going on picnics, swimming, and riding your bikes, but you need an education.

Prayers also contain wants and needs. It isn't easy deciding which are wants and which are needs. Fortunately, God sorts them out and sometimes gives you both. It's okay to eat Girl Scout cookies, as long as I remember to eat other foods as well. It's also okay to pray for what you want along with what you need. God decides which is which and what to give you.

16

BEING REAL

My strength will always be with him, my power
will make him strong.

I will love him and be loyal to him; I will make
him always victorious.

He will say to me, "You are my father and my
God."

(Ps. 89:21, 24, 26)

"'What is real?' asked the rabbit one day. . . .
"Real isn't how you are made. It's a thing that
happened to you. When a child loves you for a long,
long time. . . . Generally, by the time you are real,
most of your hair has been loved off and your eyes
drop out. But these things don't matter at all,

because once you are real, you can't be ugly, except to people who don't understand."
(Margery Williams, *The Velveteen Rabbit*)

You might recognize that quote from *The Velveteen Rabbit*. It describes many of your favorite friends—the bear that goes everywhere with you, or the stuffed dog or lamb or ragdoll that sleeps with you. You can always tell when it's a favorite friend because its fuzz isn't so fuzzy anymore, or it has lost a lot of hair and it might not be as clean as it once was. It looks worn, but it still has a special place in your heart. The doll or stuffed animal that sits on a shelf and doesn't become worn isn't doing its job of being a special friend and companion.

The Velveteen Rabbit became real only after he was loved for a very long time. Being worn was his proof of being real. You, too, become real when you are loved and when you love others. You need to get down off the shelf and sometimes even get dirty doing God's work. You can become worn out from loving. It isn't always easy loving others, and God wants you to be worn out at times. Being worn out may be proof that you are really doing what God wants—loving others.

When you become tired and worn out from loving others, God steps in and gives you new energy. He reminds you that his love makes you real and that, like your favorite teddy bear or doll, he is with us always.

EASTER

17

GOOD NEWS!

Since you are God's dear children, you must try to be like him. Your life must be controlled by love, just as Christ loved us and gave his life for us as a sweet-smelling offering and sacrifice that pleases God.

(Eph. 5:1–2)

My family had news that was too good to be true! My son Paul, who was in the Army, came home from the war in Saudi Arabia the day before Easter. The first thing I did was hug him, then I called my mother and all my sisters and brothers and my friends. I just had to share the wonderful news that Paul had come home safely. You know that news that is too good to be true just has to be shared!

It was so wonderful also because it was Easter. Christ's resurrection brought news that was too good to be true. The disciples rushed to share the news with their friends and families that Christ was risen from the dead. Easter needs to be the same for us too. We need to feel the same excitement at the sharing of the wonderful news of Christ's resurrection.

How do we share the good news of Easter? We could pick up the phone and call everyone we know. But the apostle Paul had a better idea. He gave us instructions for how to tell others about the risen Lord by living our lives a little bit differently and showing others through our lives how this good news has changed us.

Paul told us to:

Bear with one another's failings—which means if your brother or sister hits you, you don't hit him or her back.

Endure, encourage, seek unity—you do this all the time when you smile, give someone a hug, or welcome someone.

Accept one another—invite the new kid on your street or in your class to play with you. Make a new friend of someone you don't know.

Instruct one another—perhaps you can help your younger brother or sister or a friend learn how to do something.

Pray without ceasing—look for new ways to say "Thank you" to God.

Rejoice always—that's not hard for you, kids, but remember the number one enemy of rejoicing is whining.

Carry each other's burdens—help others, even when they don't ask for it.

Be humble, gentle and patient.

Wait, learn to be content—sometimes that's a hard lesson. Children want to be older than they are, adults want to be younger. God has his own timing and when we learn to make his timing our own, we can be content with our lives.

Be watchful and thankful—what are we watching for? Opportunities to share the great news that Christ is alive, he has risen from the dead, and our lives have been forever changed by this good news.

(Paraphrase of Col. 3:12–17)

18

THE EASTER CAVE

For our life is a matter of faith, not of sight.

(2 Cor. 5:7)

Have you ever been somewhere that is really, really dark? Where there is no light at all, no stars, or city lights, or even a watch that glows in the dark? Have you ever been in a cave?

When I was a child, my family visited the Carlsbad Caverns in New Mexico. We took a guided tour through this very large cave. At one point on the tour, we sat in a huge room several miles underground, and the tour guide turned off the lights to show us what real darkness was. It was so dark that I could not see my hand held in front of my face just inches from my eyes. I knew that my hand was there, even though I could not see it.

Faith is like that experience in the dark cave. Faith means that you know or believe something even though you cannot see it. I knew my hand was there even though I couldn't see it. You know that when you walk into a dark room and turn on the light that there will be light, even though you cannot see the electricity that makes that light bulb light up. You have faith that it will work even when you can't see it or understand it.

Caves were an important part of Jesus' life. He was born in one, and he was buried in one. Faith allows you to believe that the baby lying in the manger in a cave is the Son of God. Faith also helps you know that what Jesus promised came true: He is no longer in the cave where he had been buried. You can believe without seeing because of the invisible power of faith.

19

THE TRINITY

In the beginning, when God created the universe, the earth was formless and desolate.

(Gen. 1:1)

Before the world was created, the Word already existed; he was with God, and he was the same as God. . . . The Word became a human being and, full of grace and truth, lived among us.

(John 1:1, 14)

And I myself will send upon you what my Father has promised.
But when the Holy Spirit comes upon you, you will be filled with power.

(Luke 24:49; Acts 1:8)

The church has a mystery that even adults have trouble understanding. It's called the Trinity. We are taught that God is both one and three persons at the same time. He is one God, but he is also God the Father, Jesus the Son, and the Holy Spirit. There is another way I like to think about this idea that makes it easier to understand.

One way to think of the Trinity is to take three pieces of yarn. You could use all three pieces separately, one to knit a scarf, one to tie a bow on a package, and the third to tie your hair in a ponytail. Or you can take all three pieces and braid them. They are still three pieces of yarn, but now, braided, they are one.

Think about a father. He is his parents' son and a father to his children and a husband to his wife. One person with three roles.

It is very hard to understand God completely. But it helps to think of the roles he plays in your life. God, the Father, the Creator reminds you of your own father. But what if you had a father who wasn't always loving and caring and providing for you? Even if you didn't know your human father or have one who isn't as loving as God, you can still understand God as a Father if you think about the best father you know.

Jesus, the Son, was the gift of the Father, sent to bring you the promise of eternal life with the Father. God became a man, Jesus, so that you could know and understand God better because he faced the same problems and temptations you do and died just as you will someday.

The Holy Spirit is the friend Jesus promised you. Jesus knew that even though he came and brought each of you the chance for a closer relationship with God, you would still have difficulties. You might forget his teachings and need help. The Holy Spirit is available to you to remind you of God's Word, to help you understand it and live it.

Three persons, one God.

20

BACK TO THE FUTURE

God said, "I am who I am. . . . This is my name forever."

(Ex. 3:14–15)

Remember the *Back to the Future* movies? The story involved someone going back in time and changing part of the past which resulted in changes in the future. Because of these changes people in the present had different personalities, and events in their lives were different. But you can't really go back in time and make changes. And it's probably a good thing you can't.

In the Old Testament, God's people had a name for him. They called him "Yahweh," which means, "I am who I am." A woman named Helen Mallicoat explained what this means.

"When you live in the past with its mistakes and regrets, it is hard. I am not there. My name is not 'I was.' When you live in the future, with its problems and fears, it is hard. I am not there. My name is not, 'I will be.' When you live in this moment, it is not hard. I am here. My name is 'I am.'"

God wants you to live in the present because you miss so many opportunities to praise him and thank him when you are feeling guilty about the past or worrying about the future. When you give him control over your clock and calendar, you let him take care of mistakes and worries.

21

A SERVANT'S HEART

Then he poured some water into a washbasin and began to wash the disciples' feet and dry them with the towel around his waist.

"I, your Lord and Teacher, have just washed your feet. You, then, should wash one another's feet. I have set an example for you, so that you will do just what I have done for you."

(John 13:5, 14–15)

Sometimes I think I am the only one living in my house who can change the toilet paper roll. And the only one who knows how to hang up a towel, close a cabinet door, and sort the laundry. That doesn't mean I like doing those things;

they're boring and unrewarding. But I learned a valuable lesson from a friend of mine who sold toilet bowl cleaner for a living. He was determined to be the best bowl cleaner and salesman. And he was, because he dedicated this part of his life to the Lord!

He was very serious about it when he told me how exciting toilet bowl cleaning became when he did it for the Lord. Can you think of anything worse than cleaning other people's toilet bowls? But my friend explained to me that whenever you do something for Christ that serves other people you are rewarded. You have the reward of knowing you are helping someone, which is a way of sharing Christ with them. And you have the reward of joining the Kingdom of God and spending eternity with God.

God calls you to be a servant for others. That might mean picking up a dropped sock, putting away the folded towels, making a sandwich for a lunch box. These aren't the most rewarding tasks, except when you do them for someone you love, in the Lord's example. Think about how you might be a servant in your home. What? You already feel like a slave! When you do something for someone else remember how the Lord served others. He washed their feet. He never grumbled or said it wasn't his turn, or even had to be asked. Serving others isn't a party, usually, but when you do it for the Lord, you will be rewarded.

22

THE RAINMAKER

Be persistent in prayer, and keep alert as you pray, giving thanks to God.

(Col. 4:2)

There once was a man whose name no one could remember, because for as long as anyone knew him he was called "Rainmaker." He traveled wherever there was a drought and before long, it would rain. No one was sure how he did it, but they knew that if there were a drought, the Rainmaker was sure to come along and when he did, it rained.

The town where Rainmaker grew up wanted to honor him for his service to others. They called a town meeting and voted that Rainmaker should be given the town's most important award, the "Person of the Year" plaque. The local newspaper reporter went to Rainmaker's home to interview him. All the facts came out quickly: where Rainmaker had been born and when and where he went to school and who his friends were. But something was missing from the reporter's story, so the reporter asked Rainmaker, "How do you make it rain?"

The Rainmaker answered, "I don't."

"But wherever you go, it rains," the reporter protested.

The Rainmaker explained what he did, "First I draw a circle on the ground. Then I stand in the circle . . ."

The reporter was anxious to finish the story and interrupted, "So you draw a circle that makes it rain."

"No," said the Rainmaker, "I draw the circle and stand in the center and I pray to God until he makes the rain fall."

The reporter couldn't believe his ears. "Do you mean God makes it rain because you draw a circle and stand in the center and pray?"

The Rainmaker answered, "No, I believe God sends the rain because of the prayer. The circle is just there to remind me to stay and pray until he washes it away."

At some point in your life, you may need to draw a circle to remind yourself to stay and pray until God answers. That circle might be written in the dirt, or it might be made by hands around the dining room table, or it might be a circle of friends gathered together. Paul reminds us to be persistent in prayer, which means if you're praying for rain, keep at it until you're all wet.

23

HAPPY BIRTHDAY!

When the day of Pentecost came, all the believers were gathered together in one place. Suddenly there was a noise from the sky which sounded like a strong wind blowing, and it filled the whole house where they were sitting. Then they saw what looked like tongues of fire which spread out and touched each person there. They were all filled with the Holy Spirit.

(Acts 2:1–4)

When is your birthday? Birthdays are important because they let us celebrate how glad we are that you were born, that you're a part of our family and that you're growing older. Having a birthday means you are a whole year older and probably a lot different than you were last year. How do you celebrate your birthday? I'll bet you have presents and a cake and candles.

Did you know the church also has a birthday? The church's birthday is a day called "Pentecost." The book of Acts tells us what happened that day. "When the day of Pentecost came, all the believers were gathered together in one place. Suddenly there was a noise from the sky which sounded like a strong wind blowing, and it filled the whole house where they were sitting. Then they saw what looked like tongues of fire which spread out and touched each person there. They were all filled with the Holy Spirit" (Acts 2:1–4).

The church's birthday is much like yours. Everyone was gathered together in the same way you invite your friends over for a party. God gave the disciples a gift, the Holy Spirit, just as you receive gifts on your special day. To show his presence, God sent tongues of flames which appeared above their heads. The candles on your cake remind us of the tongues of fire.

As you celebrate the church's birthday at Pentecost, remember to thank God for the gift of his church and that we are all growing together as a church family.

SPRING

24

THE INVISIBLE MAN

Paul wrote to his friends in Rome,

Αs the scripture says, "Those who were not told about him will see, and those who have not heard will understand."

(Rom. 15:21)

There was an old movie and a television series about a scientist who had an accident of some sort and became invisible. He went around doing things, but other people didn't know he was there because they couldn't see him. Every now and then he would become visible, usually at the worst possible moment, but then he'd fade away again just in time to get away.

Wouldn't you just love to be invisible? You could sneak a cookie and no one would see you, or you could find out what people are saying about you when you're not around. Of course, there are some disadvantages to being invisible because you could also do something nice and no one would know you did it.

Actually, that's a good idea. If you were invisible and did good things for others, they would only have God to thank for it because they wouldn't know it was you. The apostle Paul wanted very much to tell others the story of Christ's life, but he didn't want to take any credit for Christ's promise of salvation. Paul wanted people to see Christ at work in their own lives, not Paul at work for Christ. Paul wanted to become invisible so that people would look only at Christ.

You, too, can become invisible while doing God's work. There are hundreds of little chores that someone in your home does every day. You can help with them in secret, without taking credit for them. Then the other members of your family will have to thank God because they won't know it was you who helped them.

Don't you just hate it when someone catches you being naughty? The invisible man couldn't be caught doing something because he was invisible. The invisible Christian can be caught doing good, though, because even when you do something in secret, God knows. Practice being an invisible Christian and you may be caught doing good, if not by your mom or dad, then certainly by God!

25

GINGERBREAD COOKIES

We have many parts in the one body, and all these parts have different functions. In the same way, though we are many, we are one body in union with Christ, and we are all joined to each other as different parts of one body. So we are to use our different gifts in accordance with the grace that God has given us.

(Rom. 12:4–6)

Have you ever made gingerbread cookies? If you were very careful, they all came out just the same size, with two arms, two legs, and the same shaped heads. Maybe you even decorated them, painting on some clothes, or putting silver balls for eyes, nose, and mouth, or for buttons down the front. By decorating them with different colored icings you could tell them apart; otherwise they all looked alike.

It's a good thing you and I aren't gingerbread cookies. If you looked like me and I looked like you, and everyone here looked alike, how could you tell which parent to go home with? How could I tell which children belong at my house? It would be very confusing, and it would be boring if we all looked alike.

Think about how different the world would be if we all looked alike. We'd all have the same hair color and style so there wouldn't be any need for hairdressers. And clothing stores would only have to offer one size of clothing. You could turn on the TV and see someone who looked just like you doing the news and weather and then appearing on every show. The newspaper wouldn't bother printing pictures because everyone would look the same.

Thank goodness we're all different! There's no one exactly like you, even if you have an identical twin. You may look like each other, but you are unique and individual. Because you are different from everyone else in the world, you are special.

Not only are you special and unique, but you also have individual jobs in God's kingdom. Paul wrote to his friends in Rome, "We have many parts in the one body, and all these parts have different functions. In the same way, though we are many, we are one body in union with Christ, and we are all joined to each other as different parts of one body. So we are to use our different gifts in accordance with the grace that God has given us" (Rom. 12:4–6).

Be glad you are different because it is your differentness that makes you special to God, to his people, and to the church.

26

THE LOWLY PENNY

It is the LORD's blessing that makes you wealthy.
(Prov. 10:22)

In the book of Proverbs there is this advice, "It is the LORD's blessing that makes you wealthy" (10:22).

If I offered you a million dollars today, or a penny that I would double every day for a month, which would you take? Before you answer, let me explain more. Today, you would receive a penny; tomorrow, two cents; the next day, four cents. At the end of the first week, you would have sixty-four cents. Still want the million dollars?

At the end of two weeks, your doubled penny would have grown to $81.92. That million dollars still looks like the better deal, doesn't it? After three weeks, you would have $10,485.76. But that's still a long way from a million dollars. On the thirtieth day, that penny would have added up to $5,368,708.80.

God's blessings are often little and may go unnoticed, but over time, they add up to a picture of God's overwhelming love for you. The sunrise every morning, the clouds that make the sky interesting and give you shade, the rain that helps flowers grow, beautiful birds, a kitten's soft purr, a puppy's playfulness, the sticky hug of a three-year-old, and peanut butter fingerprints on the refrigerator are all little everyday blessings from God. Can you think of some little blessings in your own life? Put them all together and you will see the beautiful pattern of God's love for you.

27

SEEDS

Teach a child how he should live, and he will remember it all his life.

(Prov. 22:6)

Do you have a garden? I like to plant a garden. It seems like such a miracle that a tiny, ugly, hard seed can grow into a beautiful flower or a delicious vegetable. Not only is it a miracle, but one year it was a mystery. I had bought several packets of seeds for different vegetables and flowers, and one of my children opened all of them and poured them into a bowl. Can you imagine how confusing that was? Jesus understood seeds and gardens and used them to illustrate many lessons he taught. He talked about planting seeds on rocky soil and about weeds growing among good seed and about trees that bear fruit and those that don't, but he didn't have any parables about mixed up seeds.

I wasn't sure what I was planting so I just held my breath and waited until the plants sprouted. God provided the sun and rain, and I did my part keeping the weeds and bugs under control. When the time came to harvest, my garden looked a little strange with marigolds next to beans and onions and squash in the middle of the tomatoes. But everything turned out all right.

The seeds are like children. You started out as babies. You looked different and had different personalities. You grew at different rates. But when you were little babies, your parents had no idea what you might become. Even today, there is still a lot of mystery about what you will be like as adults. We can guess how you will look, what color your eyes and hair will be, but we don't know what you'll be like as adults.

God didn't provide gardening instructions, but he did give us parents help with our children. We have the Bible to guide us and the church to support us as we anxiously await our harvests to see what our garden holds.

28

WHERE'S WALDO?

You are like salt for all mankind. . . . You are like light for the whole world. A city built on a hill cannot be hid. . . . In the same way your light must shine before people, so that they will see the good things you do and praise your Father in heaven.

(Matt. 5:13–16)

Christ was talking to his friends and teaching them. He told them to be the "salt of the earth" and "the light of the world." He wanted them to stand out and be noticed so that other people would come to know about God through them. If he came here today, I think he'd tell you to be a "Waldo" for the world.

You know about Waldo—he is a little funny looking, and he hides in a crowd of people who all look very much alike. The only way you can find him in the picture is because he looks a little different. You just look and look until you spot him.

God doesn't necessarily want you to look different, but he does want you to stand out in the crowd. He wants others to notice you because he is in your heart. He wants you to be a Waldo for the world, for him. How can you be a Waldo? It might mean doing something that isn't the most popular thing, but you'd do it for God. For example, a Waldo would make friends with a new kid in school even if that kid dressed or talked a little differently from everyone else. A Waldo would recycle trash as a good steward of God's resources, even though it may be easier to throw a recyclable item in the regular trash can. A Waldo is a little different from others but different in a way that pleases God.

29

ACTS OF KINDNESS

But the Spirit produces love, joy, peace, patience, kindness, goodness, faithfulness, humility, and self-control.

(Gal. 5:22)

Recently I heard someone suggest that we practice random acts of kindness, which means to look for an opportunity to be kind to someone without expecting a reward, just for the sake of being kind. The Hebrew people had two words for acts of kindness. One was *mitzvah*. This meant doing something nice for someone, such as picking up something they have dropped or helping them with a task. The second type of kindness is the greatest kind of good deed. It is the *chesed.*

When you perform a *chesed,* you expect nothing in return. The person may not even deserve your kindness or even know you have done it. You do it to please God. The *chesed* gives a person a reason to celebrate the blessing of God.

Think about the many acts of kindness you can do, especially those you can do without anyone knowing you did it. For example, you could make your brother's bed when he is at school or take out the trash for your mom without being asked or reminded. You could set the table when it isn't your turn. You could bring the newspaper in for your parents or pick up a dropped shirt and put it away. The secret is to do it for the Lord without expecting anything in return, and without letting anyone know you have done a *chesed.*

SUMMER

30

THE BEAVERS

Since you have accepted Christ Jesus as Lord, live in union with him. Keep your roots deep in him, build your lives on him, and become stronger in your faith, as you were taught. And be filled with thanksgiving.

(Col. 2:6–7)

Have you ever seen beavers at work building a dam? You've probably heard they are hardworking and single-minded in their work. When they set out to build a home, they don't stop until it's done. But what do you think happens to the stream the beavers live in? I'll tell you.

Behind the small country church we used to attend, a stream lazily wound its way through a field. The stream branched out into little channels, the water barely moving in some of them. You could look into the water and see little tadpoles swimming crazily. Even after a March cloudburst, the water would only spill over the bank for a short while, then quickly settle back into its narrow bed.

One year a family of beavers moved in and began a summer-long building project. One branch of the creek wasn't large enough for the whole beaver clan so they went to work damming up several branches of the creek. They cut down small trees with their sharp teeth and dragged them to their dams. The beavers added mud and twigs and grass and leaves. Slowly the water backed up and a pond formed. Each week, we'd walk out to see how much larger the pond had grown. By August the creek was gone—all its branches had merged into a pond.

Do you ever feel like a little creek, running in so many different directions each day? At the end of the day, do you wonder what you've done with your time and energy? Jesus pulls us all together. Like the mud and sticks of the beavers, Christ provides support for you and gives your flow direction and strength. No longer are you a wandering stream. Because of Christ you have strength to reach out to others, and with Christ, your heart can overflow with love for them, just as the beavers' stream overflowed into a pond.

31

ACCIDENTS HAPPEN

God is our shelter and strength, always ready to help in times of trouble.

(Ps. 46:1)

A few years ago I had an accident. I was roller skating with my children and doing something I shouldn't have been doing—playing tag. When I leaned forward to tag one of my kids, I fell and broke my arm. Unfortunately, it was my right arm, and I am right-handed. I couldn't write or dress myself or drive my car, which had a gear shift, or even brush my teeth. I had to learn to do everything left-handed. But God used the accident to teach me to accept the help of others. My daughter helped me dress, and a friend loaned me a car that I could drive. Everyone at home pitched in and cooked and cleaned.

Even though accidents are a part of daily life, we sometimes ask God why this has happened to us, instead of trying to learn a lesson from it. You know that when you first tried to learn to skate or ride a bike, you fell down a lot. It's all part of learning how. The best way you can respond is to get up and keep on trying.

That's true of many things that happen in life. God uses accidents to teach you lessons, especially the lesson that he cares for you when you turn to him and even when you don't. God didn't cause me to fall down and break my arm, but he did use the accident to teach me to let others help me. You, too, can look for lessons in your accidents to see what God wants you to learn.

32

ARE YOU ABLE OR AVAILABLE?

I have the strength to face all conditions by the power that Christ gives me.

(Phil. 4:13)

Did you ever want to be good at something? I mean really, really good—the best basketball player or an Olympic swimmer or a gold medal winning gymnast. Perhaps there is something you're good at. Perhaps God has given you some special talent which you can practice and work on until you're the best you can be. You might have a lovely singing voice or athletic ability or maybe you can dance or write stories.

Or perhaps you are an ordinary person who enjoys sports or music, but you don't have that special talent to become the best in that area. You can still do your best and nurture that ability. The important thing to God is not your ability but your availability. He wants you to use the special gifts he has given you to do his work. And he gives you strength and talent to do his work. The apostle Paul reminds us of this in his letter to his friends at Philippi. He writes, "I have the strength to face all conditions by the power that Christ gives me" (Phil. 4:13).

In order to do the best you can for God, you must be open to him and available to him to use as he sees fit. So look for those areas where God has blessed you with special abilities. Practice, learn, and develop your gifts and talents to their fullest. Remember also that even if you're not the best, if you don't win any medals, or if you don't go to the Olympics, you're always number one with God when you make your ability available to him.

33

THE LANGUAGE OF GOD

I may be able to speak the languages of men and even of angels, but if I have no love, my speech is no more than a noisy gong or a clanging bell.

(1 Cor. 13:1)

I have friends who are missionaries in a country where Spanish is spoken. When my friends go to church they might hear someone say, *"Diós, tu adoro porque me llamo su hijo,"* which means, "God, I adore you because I am called your son."

In churches all over the world different languages are used to praise God. Some you might understand; others might seem very strange to you. But in each church the message is the same because we are all worshiping the same God. But what language do you think God understands?

God's Word says, "I may be able to speak the languages of men and even of angels, but if I have no love, my speech is no more than a noisy gong or a clanging bell" (1 Cor. 13:1).

God hears the language of love. He hears when you praise and thank him, when you encourage your friends, or give your parents a hug. He hears your special whispers of "I love you" that you don't think anyone else can hear. God hears when you love one another. That is like beautiful music to his ears, not a noisy gong or clanging bell.

34

PRAYING FOR THE LITTLE THINGS

Ask, and you will receive; seek, and you will find; knock, and the door will be opened to you. For everyone who asks will receive, and anyone who seeks will find, and the door will be opened to him who knocks. Would any of you who are fathers give your son a stone when he asks for bread? Or would you give him a snake when he asks for a fish? As bad as you are, you know how to give good things to your children. How much more, then, will your Father in heaven give good things to those who ask him!

(Matt. 7:7–11)

My friend Linda learned an important lesson about prayer one windy afternoon. She was at a park and lost her contact lens; the wind whipped it right off her finger. She and everyone with her began looking around on the ground for the lost lens. A couple passed by and asked what had been lost and if they could help. Linda explained she had dropped her contact lens and the couple stopped and began to pray that the lens would be found. After their prayer, they looked also and the lens was found. Linda was reminded that we need to drop to our knees in prayer before dropping to our knees in search of something lost. God wants us to trust him with the little things as much as we trust him with the big things.

What little things have happened in your life that you could have prayed about? Did you ever lose a pet? Or get a bad grade? Or want to play on a baseball team? Or have an argument with your best friend? Or have a sick grandpa? Or have a bad dream? All of these things can be talked over with God in prayer. He's waiting on you to turn to him, whether you have a big problem or a little one.

35

GOD'S PIGGY BANK

At that time the Kingdom of heaven will be like this. Once there was a man who was about to leave home on a trip; he called his servants and put them in charge of his property. He gave to each one according to his ability: to one he gave five thousand gold coins, to another he gave two thousand, and to another he gave one thousand. Then he left on his trip. The servant who had received five thousand coins went at once and invested his money and earned another five thousand. In the same way the servant who had received two thousand coins earned another two thousand. But the servant who had received one thousand coins went off, dug a hole in the ground, and hid his master's money.

After a long time the master of those servants came back and settled accounts with them. . . .

For to every person who has something, even more will be given, and he will have more than enough; but the person who has nothing, even the little that he has will be taken away from him.

(Matt. 25:14–19, 29)

Do you have a bank for pennies? It probably has a slot in the top for deposits and a larger hole on the bottom for withdrawals. The problem with piggy banks is you always want to take more out than you put in. Fortunately, God's bank lets you do just that! He gives you a bank full of his love. He makes all the deposits and wants you to make the withdrawals. The more love you take out and use, the more he gives you to put to work.

Jesus explained this principle in a story about a wealthy man who was about to go on a journey. He called together his servants and gave each of them some money. Two of the men invested wisely and made more money. The third man buried his money in a hole in the ground. When the wealthy man returned he asked his servants to account for how they had used the money. He was pleased with the two who used it wisely, but he punished the third man.

God wants you to use the love he gives you. When you share that love with others, you have a never-ending supply of love. God's piggy bank of love overflows. What about your parents? They don't have piggy banks; they're too old for them. Instead, they have credit cards. God gives adults a credit card with no limits on love, so long as they use it. You could even call it a "Master Card."

36

THE KITE

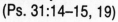

But my trust is in you, O LORD; you are my God. I am always in your care; . . . How wonderful are the good things you keep for those who honor you! Everyone knows how good you are, how securely you protect those who trust you.

(Ps. 31:14–15, 19)

When we first moved to Florida one of our delights was flying kites at the beach. Perhaps you like that too. There is a steady breeze most of the time and lots of space to fly kites. One summer my son received a kite for his birthday, and we headed for the beach to fly it. It dipped and skipped all over the sky until my son was tired of holding the string and let it go.

Do you know what happened then? The kite came crashing down. But not straight down on the sand where we were standing. Instead, it landed on the roof of a condominium near the beach.

We walked over and looked around until we spotted it on top of the roof, but we couldn't figure out a way to get it down. Finally, I noticed a repair truck down the road. A man was working on the electric lines. I walked over and asked him if he could help us, but he didn't think that would be possible since he was supposed to be fixing the wires. I explained that it would be very kind of him if he could help since it was my son's birthday and his first kite. If he could just spare a few minutes, I was sure it wouldn't take very long and my son would be very grateful. Well, the man did come down and rescued the kite for us.

My son learned a valuable lesson that day about letting go of the string and about helping others. You are like that kite. When you let Christ hold your string, you flutter and dance and sail on the wind. It's only when you pull the string out of his hand that you crash.

Sometimes a helping hand from a friend puts you back where you belong, firmly held in Christ's hand and aloft once again.

37

A SWIMMING RIBBON

Let us run with determination the race that lies before us. Let us keep our eyes fixed on Jesus, on whom our faith depends from beginning to end.

(Heb. 12:1–2)

Have you ever won a ribbon? Perhaps for a race or a science project? My mother found a letter I wrote when I was about twelve years old. I wrote it to my father who was away from home with the military. I shared with him a ribbon I had won in a swimming race. My letter is full of excitement with long descriptions about the race and about how I felt when I won! I even told my father to show my ribbon to all his friends; I was so proud of myself. My mother added a note to my letter saying she had removed the ribbon that meant so much to me from the envelope because she was afraid my father would misplace the ribbon. Apparently my mother must have told me she had taken the ribbon out because there was a second note from me where I traced the ribbon so my father would have a picture of it.

Now, thirty years later, I have these letters but no ribbon to remind me of my one and only swimming victory. I don't even remember the race now.

The apostle Paul understood athletes and the excitement of winning a race. He wrote a letter to the Hebrews about running a race and about the excitement of winning. He knew it was important to put your all into the race, avoid distraction, do your best. In Paul's race, the prize is not a ribbon or medal which can be lost and which can lose its importance with time. The prize is an eternal reward in God's kingdom.

38

OUR SOCCER BALL

Don't worry about anything, but in all your prayers ask God for what you need, always asking him with a thankful heart.

(Phil. 4:6)

Several years ago my children wanted a soccer ball, but we didn't have any extra money to buy one. They prayed every evening at dinner and at bedtime for a ball. One morning we found one on the roof of our house! We went throughout the neighborhood to be sure someone hadn't lost their ball. No one claimed it, and we decided it must be a gift from God. We enjoyed that ball for a long time, and it taught us two lessons: that God hears our prayers and that we must be prepared for his answers.

We took the ball with us on a picnic to the park one day. All my children liked a game we invented which involved kicking the ball back and forth between two teams, trying to keep it away from the other team, but without any boundaries or goals. I had worn sandals and soon my toes became bruised from the kicking. One of my daughters wore old tennis shoes and the kicking tore them up and soon her toes were hanging out too. We both went home with sore feet.

Life is often like our soccer ball game; if you're not properly prepared you can't play the game as well. God wants you to be ready and equipped to do his work. What can you do to prepare yourself for the things God wants you to do?

God will also help you become ready. You must learn to talk to him in prayer, thank him for his gifts, study his Word, and love one another. Sometimes the lessons aren't easy and you may go home with sore feet!

39

SPECIAL FRIENDS

And I will be with you always, to the end of the age.

(Matt. 28:20)

Do you have a special friend, a stuffed animal or doll that goes with you everywhere? You can talk to your special friend and tell it everything and anything. He or she just sits there and listens and never objects or interrupts. You can hug your special friend, and he thinks you're the greatest. Everyone needs a special friend.

I know someone who had such a friend and lost her but she never forgot her. My great-grandmother was in her nineties when she told me about her corncob doll. This was a doll made from a corncob dressed with bits of cloth for clothing. She didn't have a face or hair, and she wasn't very cuddly, but she was the only doll my great-grand-mother ever had. Her family was too poor to buy a store-bought doll. My great-grandmother had eight younger brothers and sisters, and by the time she was old enough to take care of herself, she also had two or three babies to take care of. She sat for hours rocking the cradle or washing diapers in a tub and hanging them to dry. Even though she was a little girl, she worked very hard.

My great-grandmother's little doll went every-where with her, to the water pump to fetch a bucket of water, to the garden to pick vegetables, to the window sill to watch while she washed dishes. Her doll was a very special friend!

One night there was a fire that destroyed their log cabin and everything in it. They barely es-caped with their lives and my great-grandmother lost her doll. When she was a very old woman, she remembered that doll as if she had held it the day before. That's how special that doll was to her.

You have special friends like that to remind you of the friendship you have with Jesus. When times are good, he is there watching you, walking along-side you. When times are difficult, you can remember how close Jesus is even when it seems like he isn't there. He is a very special friend for life.

AUTUMN

40

THE APPLE TREE

Pay no attention to how tall and handsome he is. I have rejected him, because I do not judge as man judges. Man looks at the outward appearance, but I look at the heart.

(1 Sam. 16:7)

Do you ever worry about how tall you are or if you are tall enough? My sister told me a story about an apple tree who had just such worries.

The apple tree lived in a forest of pines. It was the only apple tree in the forest, and it was very lonely. In addition, the pine trees growing around it were much taller than the little apple tree and liked to tease him about his height. During the daytime, it didn't matter so much that the little apple tree was short for the sun was tricky and able to peek through the pine branches to shine on the apple tree. But the nights were very dark for the little apple tree who couldn't see past the towering pines to enjoy the stars.

The pine trees spent the whole night exclaiming, "Look how beautiful that star is!" "No, that one's much bigger and brighter." "See how the North Star twinkles at me." "The Big Dipper is my favorite."

The little apple tree reached and stretched but just couldn't see the stars. Finally, he complained to God, who listened patiently and said, "Wait; just wait. You will see the stars."

The apple tree waited. In the spring he grew beautiful fragrant blossoms and in the fall, big, juicy, red apples. But try as he might, he still couldn't see the stars and was certain he'd never grow tall like the pines. Years passed and once again, he complained to God.

God answered by picking an apple and cutting it open horizontally to show the tree a simple star within. God said, "It's not what you see that counts but what's inside you."

In the first book of Samuel, the Lord says, "Pay no attention to how tall and handsome he is. I have rejected him, because I do not judge as man judges. Man looks at the outward appearance, but I look at the heart" (16:7).

41

AMEN

When you pray, do not use a lot of meaningless words, as the pagans do, who think their gods will hear them because their prayers are long.

(Matt. 6:7)

There is a word that you use all the time in church and at home when you pray. It's at the end of prayers and some hymns. The word is *amen*. You may think this word means the end of something. At dinnertime, it means, "Okay, you can pass the food now." At church it means, "I can stop looking at my shoes now because the quiet time is over." Or perhaps you think it means, "Great, we don't have to sing anymore and I can sit down now."

Amen has much more meaning than we give it. It comes from the Hebrew language which Christ spoke and it means "certainly" or "so be it." The Hebrews used the word when they wanted to express their agreement with something someone was saying or their hope that the statement would become true. On "Star Trek: The Next Generation," the captain frequently tells his officers, "Make it so." That's what *amen* means.

Amen after a hymn adds your agreement that what you have just sung is true. You'd better pay closer attention to the words you're singing! *Amen* adds your hope to a prayer that the prayer will be answered. However, many times when you pray you have an idea exactly how those prayers should be answered. Then *amen* says, "This is what I want and how I want it."

God might have another plan for you. Perhaps his answer is different from yours, or his timing includes waiting for an answer. When you pray, your *amen* needs to say, "Lord, do it your way and make your way my way, too." Then when you add, "Amen," it will really say, "Make it so!"

42

LOOKING BACK/LOOKING AHEAD

Future generations will serve him; men will speak of the Lord to the coming generation. People not yet born will be told: "The LORD saved his people."

(Ps. 22:30–31)

Have you ever asked your parents what their life was like when they were your age? I don't mean in a smart, "Did they have the wheel then?" way. If you ask your parents about life when they were kids you might be surprised by their answers. In the 1960s when most of them were your age, there was a war in a country on the other side of the world, Vietnam. Many of your parents or their family or friends were involved either in military service or in protests against the war. Lyndon Johnson was president of the United States then, and interest rates and inflation were both high.

Ronald Reagan was the governor of California. Walt Disney died in the sixties, and the first heart transplant took place. Young people were called "hippies." There were no home computers, Nintendo, pocket calculators, or DisneyWorld. On television your parents watched "Perry Mason," "The Donna Reed Show," "The Andy Williams Show," "Rawhide," "The Flintstones," "My Three Sons," "The Andy Griffith Show," "Gomer Pyle, U.S.M.C.," "Bonanza," "The Virginian," "The Beverly Hillbillies," "Petticoat Junction," "Bewitched," "Green Acres," "The Dick Van Dyke Show," "Mission Impossible," and "Laugh-in." There was one show that began in the late sixties and almost didn't have a second season because its ratings were so low—"Star Trek."

Your parents listened mostly to AM radio stations because FM wasn't popular yet. Their favorite musicians were Petula Clark, the Supremes, Herman's Hermits, the Rolling Stones, the

Beatles, Sonny and Cher, the Association, the Mamas and Papas, the Beach Boys, Simon and Garfunkel, and, of course, Frank Sinatra.

Their favorite songs might have been: "Cherish," "Last Train to Clarksville," "You Can't Hurry Love," "Sounds of Silence," "Monday, Monday," "California Dreamin'," "Ballad of the Green Berets," and "Strangers in the Night."

Once you get your parents reminiscing, it may be hard to stop them! Their youth seems like a long time ago to you and very different from now. But, every Sunday, people went to church and Sunday school. The choir practiced, and the youth group met. Parents brought their children to church. Those children grew up, and now they bring you, their children, to church.

What do you think life will be like when you become parents and bring your children to church? Will you drive a car or some other kind of vehicle? Will computers be in every home? Will your children watch today's television shows as reruns? Will they think your music is weird? Will Sunday school still teach your children? Will the choir still sing and the youth group still meet? Will you be one of the leaders of your church?

The Bible says, "Future generations will serve him; men will speak of the Lord to the coming generation. People not yet born will be told: 'The LORD saved his people'" (Ps. 22:30–31).

I am thankful for the people who became your parents, who are teaching you about the Lord, so that one day you can teach your children.

43

LITTLE BLESSINGS

Many rich men dropped in a lot of money; then a poor widow came along and dropped in two little copper coins, worth about a penny. He called his disciples together and said to them, "I tell you that this poor widow put more in the offering box than all the others. For the others put in what they had to spare of their riches; but she, poor as she is, put in all she had—she gave all she had to live on."

(Mark 12:41–44)

Did you ever find a penny lying on the ground? I find them frequently because I watch for them when I am walking. I am surprised that so many people don't think pennies have any value. I always pick them up and save them in a jar. Pretty soon they add up.

Jesus reminds us of the value of a penny. One day while he was sitting in the temple area, people were passing him to give their money offerings. "Many rich men dropped in a lot of money; then a poor widow came along and dropped in two little copper coins, worth about a penny. He called his disciples together and said to them, 'I tell you that this poor widow put more in the offering box than all the others. For the others put in what they had to spare of their riches; but she, poor as she is, put in all she had—she gave all she had to live on'" (Mark 12:41–44).

A found penny reminds me of God's blessings. Sometimes you miss them because you're not looking in the right direction. Sometimes they require a little effort on your part. You have to pick them up just like that penny lying on the ground. You, too, are like the penny. Do you ever feel like you can't do much for God because you are young or little? That's not the way God sees it! When you pick up God's little blessings and share them with others, you return to God the best of offerings. Can you think of any found blessings you can share?

44

GREETINGS!

From Paul and Timothy, servants of Christ Jesus—

To all God's people in Philippi who are in union with Christ Jesus, including the church leaders and helpers: May God our Father and the Lord Jesus Christ give you grace and peace.

(Phil. 1:1–2)

It happens every day. Hundreds of times a day, without your really thinking about it, you say, "Hi!" Did you ever stop and think about why you say "Hi!" and what that means? Usually the person you greet doesn't have to do anything to deserve your greetings. They're just there.

Paul wrote a letter to his friends in a city called Philippi. Because some of his friends were Greek and others were Hebrew, he wrote two different greetings: "Charis and Shalom," which mean, in English, "Grace and peace."

Grace. It is a gift from God, freely given to you even though you don't deserve it. Grace is God's way of greeting you, his "hello." When you say "hi" or "hello" to someone, if you are sincere, the other person knows you're happy to see him or her. When God greets you with his grace, you know that he is happy to be with you.

Peace. This is also a gift from God that comes to you when you understand God's grace and his presence with you. God's peace lets you curl up in front of the fireplace when there's a blizzard blowing outside. You feel warm and snug in the midst of storms because you know God is with you.

"Charis and Shalom!" "Grace and peace!" God's special greeting to you, letting you know he is happy to be with you. So, remember when you say "hello" to someone, also let them know how happy you are to be with them.

45

GET A JOB!

One of God's favorite people, a shepherd boy named David, understood this when he wrote a song which said:

> Teach me your ways, O LORD; make them known to me. Teach me to live according to your truth, for you are my God, who saves me. I always trust in you.
>
> (Ps. 25:4–5)

Do you like to write notes to people? I like to write them to my children. I might write about something they have done which has pleased me, or perhaps about something I'd like for them to do.

Sometimes I ask their advice because one of the things I love about children is your wisdom. On one such occasion of note-exchanges, I asked my eleven-year-old daughter what she thought it meant to "wait on the Lord."

She answered me with a note that read, "I think it means waiting till he tells you your purpose in life. Susanna Wesley did."

(If you haven't heard of her, Susanna Wesley was the mother of John Wesley, who founded the Methodist Church, and of Charles Wesley, a great hymn writer.)

I wrote another note to my daughter, pushing the issue a little further. "What do you do while you're waiting?"

She answered, "Wait."

"Not fair!" I protested in my next note. "How long do you wait?"

"As long as it takes. While you're waiting, get a job. Grandma Moses, the famous American painter, didn't find her real talent until she was seventy-three."

I asked next, "When do you stop waiting?"

"Whenever God tells you," she wrote back.

"How do you know God is telling you something?" was my next question.

She explained, "You'll know. He'll communicate with you in some way."

I summarized our exchange of notes, "So, I am supposed to wait and wait and wait, and even get a job while I wait. Then when God does talk, I'll know. Then what?"

My daughter was sure of her next answer. "You do what God says!"

We adults try to make life so complicated. We ask God the same questions over and over. What do you want me to do, Lord? How can I be certain I am doing your will? What does it mean to wait upon the Lord? Because of your simple faith, you children know most of the answers. You do what God tells you, when he tells you, without asking so many questions. You know that the job God wants you to do is be yourself, waiting on him to show you what he wants you to grow into.

46

FOOTBALL

So stand ready, with truth as a belt tight around your waist, with righteousness as your breastplate, and as your shoes the readiness to announce the Good News of peace. At all times carry faith as a shield; for with it you will be able to put out all the burning arrows shot by the Evil One. And accept salvation as a helmet, and the word of God as the sword which the Spirit gives you.

(Eph. 6:14–17)

Almost everyone who was born in Columbus, Ohio, is a football fan, and I am no exception. My whole family is crazy about football. My brothers played high school football and coached younger kids when they were out of school. They also played football every Thanksgiving in a game that was called the "Turkey Bowl." That name didn't refer to the holiday, but to the players. They were two teams of grown men out to kill each other because they wore no protective gear.

Every year someone got hurt. My brother had a concussion one year and other players broke bones, injured knees, bruised and pulled muscles. As the players grew older, the injuries increased until their wives put an end to the game. Tackle football is not a game for weekend athletes and should never be played without protective gear such as helmets, shoulder and knee pads, and special shoes.

In the Bible, Paul wrote about running races and winning athletic contests. He understood the importance of the proper clothing for the job. Do you know what Paul suggested the Christian wear? You may find it a little strange, just as someone who doesn't understand football would think those uniforms and protective gear are strange. Paul's outfit for Christians included: "Truth as a belt tight around your waist, with righteousness as your breastplate, and as your shoes the readiness to announce the Good News of peace. At all times carry faith as a shield; for with it you will be able to put out all the burning arrows shot by the Evil One. And accept salvation as a helmet, and the word of God as the sword which the Spirit gives you" (Eph. 6:14–17).

Remember, when you play sports, always be prepared and use the proper gear. God wants you to do no less in your Christian life as well. By being prepared and using truth, righteousness, readiness to serve, faith, salvation, and the Word of God, you can play in God's game.

47

COUNT ME IN

Your God, the LORD himself, will be with you.
He will not fail you or abandon you.

(Deut. 31:6b)

A group of children wrote letters to God. One read, "Dear God, Count me in. Yours, Irving."

I wonder if Irving was thinking about Noah's ark and hoped that if there were a great flood again, he'd be on the boat. Or perhaps Irving thought of God as a football coach and wanted to be chosen for the first-string team. Whatever Irving's understanding of God, Irving knew for certain he wanted to be on God's side, part of his family, included in his kingdom.

What does it mean to be "counted in"? First, you'd have to have your hand held high, calling out to God, "Here I am! Don't overlook me. I want to be on your team."

It takes a lot of courage to volunteer because it means letting God be in charge. And once you're "counted in," what does that mean? Does that mean God can count on you too? That he can expect you to do your best?

Like Irving, you might be sure what you have volunteered for or what God expects of you. And like Irving, your letter could be signed, "Yours," because once you ask God to count you in, you are his. The Bible says, "Your God, the LORD himself, will be with you. He will not fail you or abandon you" (Deut. 31:66).

What would you write if you were sending a letter to God? Would you send him a thank-you note, or perhaps a long, long letter all about yourself? Maybe you'd ask a lot of questions: Is there really a pot of gold at the end of the rainbow? What ever happened to Jesus' father Joseph? How many wise men were there? What would you ask God?

Even though Irving's letter is short, it says all you ever need to say to God.

"Dear God, count me in. Yours."

48

LIVING
WATER

In Samaria he came to a town named Sychar, which was not far from the field that Jacob had given to his son Joseph. Jacob's well was there, and Jesus, tired out by the trip, sat down by the well. It was about noon. A Samaritan woman came to draw some water, and Jesus said to her, "Give me a drink of water. . . ."

The woman answered, "You are a Jew, and I am a Samaritan—so how can you ask me for a drink?" (Jews will not use the same cups and bowls that Samaritans use.)

Jesus answered, "If you only knew what God gives and who it is that is asking you for a drink, you would ask him, and he would give you life-giving water. . . ."

"Whoever drinks this water will get thirsty again, but whoever drinks the water that I will give him will never be thirsty again."
(John 4:5–10, 13–14)

A glass of water straight from the faucet usually looks clear, but there's more there than just water. There are chemicals that have been added to our water to make it safe to drink. In some areas, fluoride is added to protect teeth against decay. There are natural minerals in water that come from the ground where the water was. Some of these minerals actually help your bones grow strong. If you could look at a drop of water in a microscope, you would see tiny organisms swimming around. Most of these are harmless, and you don't even know they're there when you drink the water. Your bodies need water to live. You can go for days without food but not long at all without water.

Jesus told the woman at the well about the living water. The water he offers is living, not because it has tiny organisms swimming in it, not because it helps your bones or teeth, not because it can keep you from dying of thirst. The water Jesus offers gives eternal life. It is a water that strengthens you and protects you, and unlike a glass of water, when you drink of Jesus' living water, you will never thirst again.

49

A PLAN

I alone know the plans I have for you, plans to bring you prosperity and not disaster, plans to bring about the future you hope for.

(Jer. 29:11)

Do you know anyone who makes lists? Does your mom write one out for a trip to the grocery store? Does she keep track of Christmas gifts or cards? Does she have a calendar near the telephone to write important dates? Does she have a planner in her purse?

If there is such a thing as being overorganized, I probably am. I make lists for everything—for vacation packing, Christmas gifts, Saturday chores, shopping, party guests, telephone numbers, and even lists of my lists. I write everything down and then never throw the lists away. You never know when you might need that list again!

Lists, menus, and calendars all help me keep track of the day-to-day events I need to remember. Without the calendar and the datebook, I'd forget doctors' appointments. Without the grocery list I wouldn't know what to buy for the week. Lists help keep my life straight and my household running smoothly.

God makes lists as well. John mentions the Book of Life in Revelation, and Paul goes as far as to list several people whose names are in the Book of Life. I know God makes lists because the Bible says, "I alone know the plans I have for you, plans to bring you prosperity, not disaster, plans to bring about the future you hope for" (Jer. 29:11).

Isn't it wonderful that God has plans for your future? What happens to you isn't just fate; it can't be seen in the stars or foretold in a horoscope. God has plans only he knows for your life. He knows what's best for you, and his plan gives you a future with hope. He won't ever forget you or lose his lists. Your name is in the Book of Life.

50

ROAD MAP

After they had eaten, Jesus said to Simon Peter, "Simon son of John, do you love me more than these others do?"

"Yes, Lord," he answered, "you know that I love you."

Jesus said to him, "Take care of my lambs." A second time Jesus said to him, "Simon son of John, do you love me?"

"Yes, Lord," he answered, "you know that I love you."

Jesus said to him, "Take care of my sheep." A third time Jesus said, "Simon son of John, do you love me?"

Peter became sad because Jesus asked him the third time, "Do you love me?" and so he said to him, "Lord, you know everything; you know that I love you!"

Jesus said to him, "Take care of my sheep. I am telling you the truth: when you were young, you used to get ready and go anywhere you wanted to; . . . Follow me!"

(John 21:15–19)

Did you ever have to give someone directions to your house, but you weren't sure of the street names or how far it was from one point to another? It seems easy to find your own house but so hard to tell someone else how to find it. If you were coming to visit me I would tell you to go down the road until you see a gas station. It used to be a Texaco but now it's something else; I forget what. Then turn left and go down the street for five or six streets and turn right. Then go to the second street and turn right again. My house is on the left when the street curves, and it's the only yellow and white one unless someone else paints theirs the same color as mine. It has grass in the yard and a couple of trees and a mailbox, but then again, so does every house on my street.

Could you find my house from these directions? If you got the right start on the very first road, maybe, but probably not. I could help you by drawing a map, or better yet, I could get you a map of the whole city and show you where my house is on the map. Then you would have all the street names and directions. You could even find railroad tracks, the river, parks, schools, hospitals, and the airport to help you locate your destination.

God gave you a wonderful road map for your lives, the Bible. There are details written for you to help you. Simon Peter, too, wondered about how to follow Christ and was surprised when Christ asked him, "Simon son of John, do you love me more than these others do?"

"Yes, Lord," he answered, "you know that I love you."

Jesus said to him, "Take care of my lambs."

A second time and a third time Christ asked Simon Peter the same question, "Do you love me?" And Simon Peter answered the same both times. Finally, Christ said, "Follow me!"

The directions seem so difficult sometimes but they're really very simple, "Follow me." Like "Follow the Leader," you can follow Christ, stepping where he stepped, imitating his actions, until the day when you become like him and you arrive at your destination.

51

SECRETS

For God loved the world so much that he gave his only Son, so that everyone who believes in him may not die but have eternal life.

(John 3:16)

Do you ever find notes in your lunch bag? Sometimes I stick in love notes to my children reminding them how special they are to me and that I am thinking of them. Once I had to go out of town and when I arrived at my hotel I found a note written on a napkin in my suitcase. It said, "7 + 8 + 9 + 24." I wondered all weekend what that message meant. When I got home, my six-year-old daughter explained: She didn't know how to write "I love you, Mom," so she wrote the numbers instead.

Many families have special ways of telling each other they are loved. My mother used to pull on her earlobe. I remember being in the eighth grade spelling bee and being very nervous until I looked across the audience and saw my mother pulling on her earlobe. I knew she loved me and that gave me the confidence to spell the next word.

With my own children, I use the sign language "I love you." I hold up my right hand and stick out the thumb to the side and extend the first and fourth fingers. Now, when we are out in public and I can't say, "I love you," I can show my children this sign and they know how I feel.

God is like that too. He sends you love signs all the time, but sometimes you just don't know that's what they are, like the message in my suitcase. For example, a rainbow or a beautiful sunset or a cuddly kitten can remind you of God's precious gift of love. Can you think of any special ways God tells you about his love for you? Look around you and see if you can catch God trying to share his secret "I love you."

There is a verse in the Bible that also reminds you of God's love for you. "For God loved the world so much that he gave his only Son, so that everyone who believes in him may not die but have eternal life" (John 3:16).

52

WAITING ON GOD

Be glad, earth and sky! Roar, sea, and every creature in you; be glad, fields, and everything in you! The trees in the woods will shout for joy when the LORD comes to rule the earth.

(Ps. 96:11–13)

One of my favorite times of the year is spring because of all the lovely spring flowers that grow in Ohio, where I grew up. We had tulips, hyacinths, crocuses, jonquils, lilies, and lilacs in our yard. We'd wait all winter for the first hint of color of the flowers coming alive in the brown, dead yard. Some years they'd even come up and bloom through the snow. Finding the first flower of spring gave us hope that soon warm weather would come.

Most of these spring flowers come from hard, ugly, brown bulbs that look a little like an onion, but are hard like nuts. They are planted in the fall and must survive freezing temperatures in hard ground.

Did you ever feel like your heart is a hard, ugly flower bulb? Perhaps you've had a difficult day or been upset over something. But then, if you can give the burdens on your heart to God, he will take them and plant them like the bulbs. Then together you and God wait for the time of blossoming. That isn't always easy. You want to snatch back your worries and hold on to your anger a little longer. Have you ever tried to trust the Lord to take care of something, but then thought you could do so much better taking care of it yourself? It isn't easy to wait on the bulbs. You want to see the flowers right away. You want to have warm weather once again.

Then one day, usually when you least expect it, the spring does come. Your prayers are answered, your waiting is over. Your hard heart bursts into blossom with surprising, little, colorful flowers. You may have even forgotten you and God planted those bulbs. You may have begun to wonder if spring would ever come and the earth would be green and fresh and beautiful again.

Spring brings to mind the Psalm that your heart wants to sing again: "Be glad, earth and sky! Roar, sea, and every creature in you; be glad, fields, and everything in you! The trees in the woods will shout for joy when the LORD comes to rule the earth" (96:11–13).

About the Author

I juggle many roles every day as a mother, nurse, church school educator, and author, but my favorite role has to be a mother. Remembering how I exclaimed so many times as my children were growing up, "This has to be the best age," I now believe that every age is best, and I have children of almost every age. My oldest two are young adults, exploring their futures in business and college. The next two teens are in high school, and my youngest is in elementary school, on the threshold of teenage. They are wonderful people from whom I draw much inspiration as I write and plan messages for the Children's Moments, a regular part of worship services in our church.

My education includes a diploma in nursing from Mt. Carmel School of Nursing in my hometown, Columbus, Ohio, and a Bachelor's in history from Eastern Kentucky University in Richmond, Kentucky. I am a transplanted Ohioan, enjoying the year-round summer in Florida, where I am employed as a registered nurse and free-lance writer. Publications include a book, *A Special Kind of Parenting,* dealing with parenting handicapped children, and numerous articles in nursing journals and popular magazines.

Most of my activities and interests involve family pursuits: judging the annual district science fairs, starting a sixth-grade environmental club, taking my daughters hiking in the Yucatan peninsula of Mexico, teaching the fifth- and sixth-grade Sunday school class, and singing in the church choir.